IMAGES OF Nuneaton

WEEKLY Tribune
1895-1995

IMAGES OF Nuneaton

The Breedon Books
Publishing Company
Derby

First published in Great Britain by
The Breedon Books Publishing Company Limited
Breedon House, 44 Friar Gate, Derby, DE1 1DA.
1995

ISBN 1 85983 040 4

Printed and bound by Butler & Tanner Limited, Selwood Printing Works, Caxton Road, Frome, Somerset.

Colour separations by Colour Services, Wigston, Leicester.

Jacket printed by Premier Print, Nottingham.

Contents

Introduction

To encapsulate the life of Nuneaton in depth over a century in one book, is an impossible task.

Many other publications have covered various aspects of the town's history in words and pictures.

Images of Nuneaton is a fleeting pictorial glance at the changing places and faces of a community at work, at war and at play.

The *Trib* has been Nuneaton's bible since 1895 and we open its archives to mark 100 years of publication.

Roger Jeffery
Editor
Tribune
October 1995

It Happened In...

1895 – The *Tribune* first published.
1915 – Nuneaton Trent Valley Station rebuilt for third time.
1917 – Nuneaton railway marshalling yards handling 90,000 wagons per week.
1918 – Lt Knox VC and Cpl Beesley VC receive Freedom of the Borough.
1920 – Nuneaton Courtaulds factory opens.
1921 – Miners' strike.
1924 – Seven killed in a bus fire disaster near Cock and Bear pub; Nuneaton receives its first adequate fresh water supply.
1925 – New dole office opens in Leicester Road.
1927 – Queen Mary visits Arbury Hall and Astley Castle.
1928 – Manor Park School opened; Weddington Hall demolished; Coventry Street widened; old Nags Head pub demolished.
1929 – New Nags Head pub opened.
1930 – George Eliot Fellowship formed; Nuneaton's first carnival.
1931 – Swinnerton School opened; disastrous floods in town centre reach depth of five feet; Attleborough Hall demolished; Borough of Nuneaton receives Arms and Crest; Mr Henry Lester presents the borough with a mace.
1934 – HRH the Prince of Wales comes to Nuneaton; New Council House in Coton Road opened; Library moves from Coton Road to Queens Road; The Pheasant Inn in Abbey Street closed; Weddington Grove Hotel opens.
1935 – First clearance of slums in Abbey Street.
1939 – Arbury and Higham Lane Schools established.
1940 – First air raid in Nuneaton kills three people and injures six; Nuneaton water fountain in Market Place demolished to make standpipe for fire crews.
1941 – One hundred people killed in Nuneaton air raid.
1942 – King George VI and Queen Elizabeth inspect Civil Defence Corps; air raid in Manor Court area with 18 killed and 30 injured.
1952 – Middlemarch County Junior Schools opens.
1953 – Garden of Memory next to Riversley Park opens.
1954 – Caldwell Junior School opens.
1956 – Central bus station opens in Harefield Road; Alderman Smith Secondary School, Camp Hill Junior School, Friary County Secondary School and Red Deeps Special School open; Board Inn, Market Place, calls time and shuts up shop.
1958 – Heart in Hand pub in Wheat Street demolished.
1959 – Nuneaton flour mills finish grinding corn; Black Horse Inn in Wheat Street closed down.
1960 – Kings Head pub in Church Street demolished.
1962 – White Swan pub in Market Street closes; Nuneaton's new public library in Church Street opens.
1963 – Old Graziers Arms demolished.
1966 – Four die in Co-op Hall tragedy; Newdegate Arms Hotel closes.
1967 – Awson Carriage Works in Meadow Street scene of Nuneaton's biggest fire since the war.
1968 – Hippodrome Theatre, which was closed in mid-50s, destroyed by fire.
1974 – Nuneaton Borough Council and Bedworth Urban District Council merge into one authority.
1975 – Six people die in major train crash at Trent Valley Station.
1994 – Queen visits Nuneaton to officially open George Eliot Hospital development.

Nuneaton in the days of George Eliot. In the centre is the Market Place showing the Peacock Inn, Haddons the grocers, which is next to Market House, built in 1818 with its clock and bell tower.

The Birth of the Borough

Nuneaton gained the status of a borough in 1907 – six years after Mr W.T.Bates, at a meeting of the Urban District Council, suggested it was time the town applied for a Charter.

Mr F.S.Clay, the Clerk to the Council, told members there would be several advantages of being a borough, particularly the ability of the local authority to borrow money on more favourable terms than a district council.

But it was not until April 1904, that an agreement was reached for the sum of £350 to be put aside to cover the cost of preparing and presenting a petition for the Charter.

On May 3 of that year a public meeting was held in the new Drill Hall when it was unanimously agreed that a petition should be presented to His Majesty King Edward VII for the granting of a Charter.

On January 31, 1906, at the Council House in Queen's Road, the Honourable Everard Fielding, Barrister-at-Law and Commissioner, held an inquiry in connection with the petition, which was duly granted, after no objections were received.

Charter Day celebrations were held on a fine September Saturday in 1907 when a grand procession gathered on the Recreation Ground, led by mounted police under Superintendent Evans.

The route covered the greater part of Nuneaton and Attleborough with martial music being played by Nuneaton Town Band, Stockingford Brass Band, Coton Church Lads' Brigade Bugle Band and the Band of the 1st Battalion Royal Warwickshire Regiment.

On the arrival at the Grammar School field the Charter was read, the National Anthem played, cannons were fired and the bells of St Nicolas Church rang out.

Attractions included dancing and entertainment and in the evening 8,000 fairy lights lit up the field.

Later there followed a magnificent display of fireworks – "the latest products of pyrotechny".

Nuneaton lights up with a fireworks display on September 28, 1907, to mark the granting of its Charter as a borough town.

Alderman J.F.Johnson JP, in the Mayor's carriage as he drives through the streets of the town.

Town Clerk Mr F.S.Clay MBE, reads the Charter at the celebrations on the Grammar School field.

Bakers from Nuneaton Co-operative Society join in the carnival atmosphere.

The Charter procession winds its way along Edward Street.

Nuneaton Engineering Company on their horse-drawn tableau.

Abbey Street is packed for the procession.

Fifty years on and members of the Borough Council lead Nuneaton's Golden Jubilee celebrations. Seated (left to right): Aldermen G.Comley, W.R.Chamberlain, W.S.Johnson, H.J.Deeming, His Worship the Mayor Councillor R.Wilkinson, Aldermen C.J.S.Dickens, C.H.Cartwright, P.Woodward and R.Hadden. Second row: Councillors H.Deans, S.Williams, F.B.J.Warr, Mrs L.Whetstone, H.A.Corbett, Mrs M.J.Jarman, H.Cox, Alfred Wilkinson and L.D.Bosworth. Third row: Councillors E.W.Daffern, R.A.Moore, J.W.Lee, G.W.Pluck, M.R.Moreton, F.J.Fathers, L.Ford, E.S.Reekie, F.Thomas and H.J.Wood.

Senior officers of the Borough Council in 1957. Standing (left to right): Deputy Borough Treasurer J.W.Kay, Chief Public Health Inspector K.P.Llewellyn, Macebearer A.Broadhurst, deputy Town Clerk D.W.Cross, Housing Manager A.D.Salkeld. Seated: deputy Medical Officer of Health Dr G.Hird, Borough Treasurer E.J.Lewis, former Town Clerk T.Oldroyd, Town Clerk A.A.Crabtree, Borough Surveyor G.Ashton, Borough Education Officer R.Hargreaves, and Librarian and Curator of Art Gallery S.H.Barlow.

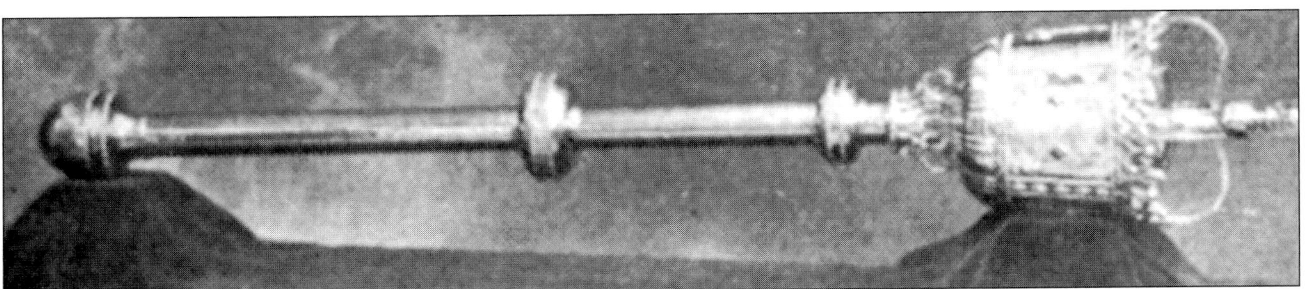

Nuneaton's mace which was presented to the Borough Council in June 1932 by Mr Henry Lester, who was in his 86th year. The mace, which is of solid silver covered with gilt, is 3ft 6in in length and weighs 112oz.

George Eliot Country

Nuneaton is George Eliot country, the birthplace of the greatest Victorian woman writer.

Born Mary Ann Evans at South Farm, Arbury, on November 22, 1819, she moved at a few months of age to Griff House, her home for more than 20 years.

Her works include *Scenes of Clerical Life, Adam Bede, Mill on the Floss, Romola* and *Felix Holt*. *Middlemarch* and *Silas Marner* were dramatised for television, winning widespread acclaim, and her novels have gained ever-increasing popularity worldwide.

Many Nuneaton places and street names are based on George Eliot's books.

The town's hospital bears the author's name and the names of its wards are constant reminders of her books and characters. A statue by local sculptor John Letts has been erected in the town centre in her memory.

Nuneaton was also the birthplace of Michael Drayton (1563-1631), the poet friend and contemporary of Shakespeare; and just outside the boundary in Mancetter lived Robert Glover, one of the best-known martyrs of the Marian persecution.

George Fox, founder of the Quakers, was born in the neighbouring village of Fenny Drayton.

George Eliot (1819-1880) – one of the greatest novelists in the Victorian era.

South Farm, Arbury, birthplace of Mary Ann Evans at 5am on November 22, 1819. She is buried at Highgate, London, and there is a memorial stone in Poets' Corner, Westminster Abbey.

Griff House, Nuneaton, home of George Eliot for 20 years, now a hotel and restaurant. This photograph was taken in 1908 before it was converted into a County Council dairy school.

George Eliot's schoolroom in Nuneaton.

Lawyer Dempster's house as it was in Church Street, Nuneaton in *Janet's Repentence*. The stone step where the unfortunate Janet sat, shivering after midnight in her thin nightdress when her drunken husband thrust her out into "the stony street in the bitter north-east wind and darkness, the harsh wind cutting her naked feet, and driving her long hair away from her half-clad bosom."

The College for the Poor, the old Coton Workhouse in College Street, Nuneaton, pulled down when George Eliot Hospital expanded. It was where the Revd Amos administered to the inmates. "In front of him sat 'Old Maxum,' Poll Fodge, known to the magistracy of her county as Mary Higgins, Silly Jim and Mr Fitchett, once a footman in the Oldenport family, and Mrs Brick, one of the hard undying old women to whom age seems to have given a network of wrinkles as a coat of magic armour against the attacks of winters warm or cold." Amos Barton. *Scenes of Clerical Life*, (Chapter Two).

William Jaques, grandson of George Eliot's "Bob Jakin", outside the front gate of the White Cottage, Griff, in November 1971.

Mrs Kathleen Adams (hand on plinth), secretary of the George Eliot Fellowship, watches the head-covered statue of the Nuneaton-born novelist being lowered into place. John Letts (bearded) was the local sculptor commissioned for the lasting memorial.

March 1986: A large crowd gathers in Newdegate Square, Nuneaton, for the unveiling of the George Eliot statue.

Michael Drayton, Poet Laureate, born in a pyramid-shaped thatched cottage on Hartshill Green in 1563. Drayton, a friend and contemporary of Shakespeare, enjoyed fame and prosperity in the golden age of Queen Elizabeth I. He died in 1631 and is buried in Westminster Abbey.

Michael Drayton's birthplace at Hartshill, Nuneaton.

George Fox, founder of the Society of Friends (Quakers), who was born near Nuneaton at Fenny Drayton, July 1624. He died on November 13, 1690, and was buried at Bunhill Fields, London.

The monument erected to the memory of George Fox in the village of his birth, Fenny Drayton.

Grand Homes Past and Present

Nuneaton and the surrounding area could boast a number of stately homes and fine buildings in the first part of the century. Some still stand, but others have been demolished.

Arbury Hall, Nuneaton's finest stately home, where the Newdegate family has lived since the late 1500s. It was immortalised as "Cheverel Manor" by George Eliot, who was born on nearby South Farm on the estate.

The Stables at Arbury Hall with the entrance designed by Sir Christopher Wren.

The Round Towers at Stockingford, the imposing entrance to Arbury Estate, pictured in the 1950s.

Astley Castle, in the 1970s, one-time home of Lady Jane Grey, before it was damaged by fire.

Weddington Castle, a Tudor building partly castellated, which was the home of the Shawe family. It was razed to the ground in 1928.

Attleborough Hall, which stood at the junction of Attleborough Road and Highfield Road, was built by George Greenway, a Nuneaton lawyer, at the beginning of the nineteenth century. A domed observatory was later added to the imposing building. Demolished in 1932.

Caldwell Hall was originally a mill. Its name was changed from Cuttle Mill to Coton Hall before becoming Caldwell Hall.

Caldecote Hall, rebuilt in 1880, lives in history as having withstood a memorable siege during the Civil War. On August 28, 1642, it was attacked by Prince Rupert and 500 men. George Abbot, son of the Archbishop of Canterbury, who had married a daughter of Colonel Purefoy with just eight men, his mother and her maids put up a brave defence. The women charged the muskets while the men fired and pewter dishes and plates were melted down for bullets. The Royalists were beaten back but as they attempted to burn out the defenders, Mistress Purefoy pleaded for mercy and Prince Rupert relented.

Camp Hill Hall, an Elizabethan-styled building, which stood on the site of an old Roman camp in Nuneaton. Before it was demolished in 1939, it was the home of the Stubbs family, whose name survives in "Stubbs Pool" in Camp Hill Road.

Oldbury Manor, a picture taken in the early 1900s.

Places of Worship

St Nicolas Parish Church has looked over Nuneaton for centuries, witnessing many changes.

Churches and chapels of all denominations have played their role in the history of the town since the great religious divide of 1662. Baptists, Congregationalists, Presbyterians, Methodists, Zionists, Quakers and others have flourished, but in time some have declined as disagreement over doctrine caused them to split into rival factions.

At the turn of the century there was a great construction programme of churches and chapels throughout Britain. Nuneaton, with its ancient C of E churches, saw the erection of new, imposing places of worship.

One such church was Manor Court Baptist. A *Tribune* writer of the day said: "Nuneaton Baptists are amongst the most pushful of local dissenters. They worshipped for many years in the unattractive building at the corner of Meadow Street and Abbey Street. The local Baptists are remarkable for their enthusiasm and stickability."

On October 19, 1899, Reginald Stanley, one of Nuneaton's great philanthropists, was presented with a golden key to open a new church. Stanley, who died in 1914 and is buried in Oaston Road cemetery, was a Wild West pioneer and the "founder and first recorder of Helena, the capital of Montana." He had earlier paid the enormous sum of £3,600 to rebuild the imposing Wesleyan chapel at the corner of Abbey Street and Stratford Street. Thanks to the generosity of the Nuneaton industrialist, it was officially opened on April 26, 1891, the hundredth anniversary of the death of John Wesley. It was demolished in 1963. The Methodist Church in Queens Road was also demolished and the two congregations joined at a new home, St John's Methodist Church, in Abbey Street, opened on January 17, 1966.

Nuneaton's Congregational Church, now the United Reformed Church, was opened in 1904 and still stands in Coton Road.

The bombing raids during World War Two took their toll of churches. Chilvers Coton, apart from the tower, was almost completely destroyed, later to be rebuilt with the help of German prisoners-of-war. St Nicolas, the Abbey, Attleborough, the Roman Catholic, Edward Street Methodist and Manor Court Baptist Churches were all damaged.

The Primitive Methodist Church in Queens Road, which was demolished in the 1960s.

Nuneaton Wesley Church, on the corner of Abbey Street and Stratford Street, which became the victim of redevelopment in 1963.

Manor Court Baptist Church, pictured in 1907.

One of the first pictures of Nuneaton Congregational Church (now the United Reformed Church), opened in Coton Road in 1904.

An early picture of St Mary's Abbey Church which was built on the site of an earlier church. The mallet used by Charles II to lay the foundation stone of St Paul's Cathedral was also used at the Abbey Church.

Coton Parish Church, pictured the day after being hit by German bombs in 1941, and after its restoration in 1947.

German prisoners-of-war take a break during the reconstruction of Coton Parish Church.

Heinrich Schonmeyer, of Bieber-Schmelz, an expert woodcarver – one of the German PoWs who helped restore Coton Church at a cost of £20,000.

St Nicolas Parish Church before the restoration of 1975 when the galleries were taken down, the walls lime-washed and the doors removed from the pews.

The opening service of St John's Methodist Church, Abbey Street, in January 1966.

One of Nuneaton's newest places of worship, the Mosque, in Frank Street, home of the town's Muslim Society, which was opened in 1984.

Thirsty Old Town

It was perhaps because miners were a thirsty lot that Nuneaton could boast so many hostelries.

After shovelling and sweating in the bowels of the earth they would adjourn to one of the scores of drinking houses in the town.

Some of the pubs have survived – but many have disappeared as the old has made way for the new in the development of the town over the years.

Nuneaton, too, used to have its own brewery in the early part of the century which was situated between Bridge Street and Bond End.

Home brewed ales. Hundreds of barrels stacked outside Nuneaton's brewery in Bridge Street and Bond End at the turn of the century.

The old Holly Bush Inn. It was replaced with a new building in Bond Gate which became the Register Office for a few years on the corner of Leicester Road.

The Plough and Ball at Abbey Green in the late nineteenth century. It was formerly called the Golden Ball and was one of the rare thatched-roof buildings to be seen in Nuneaton. The building on the right was probably a weaver's cottage with the large upstairs window providing light for a working hand loom.

The Board Inn, Market Place, photographed in November 1956, a few months before the eighteenth-century inn was demolished and the site redeveloped for shops.

The imposing Newdegate Arms Hotel, acknowledged as one of the finest buildings in Nuneaton. Situated on the corner of Newdegate Square, it was used by businessmen and farmers, particularly on cattle market day, where many business deals were struck. It was demolished in 1966.

The "old" Newdegate Arms as it was in the early 1900s. According to the Gentleman's Journal of April 1909, it had been in existence for 400 years, covering an area of 18 acres, including a sports field and the site of the weekly stock market.

Standing in the shadow of Mount Jud, the Punch Bowl shortly before its demolition, photographed in October 1950.

The Castle Inn (left) and the Red Lion (top centre) in May 1969, two pubs in Nuneaton town centre which disappeared under a redevelopment scheme.

The Olde Wharfe Inn in Coventry Road... flattened to make way for a housing development by the canalside.

The Cock and Bear – pulled down early in the century to be replaced by another pub, bearing the same name, which stands next to the town's Manor Park football ground.

The Royal Red Gate Inn on the A5, a familiar landmark for travellers along the Watling Street.

Last orders have been called at the George and Dragon in Queens Road, Nuneaton, as it awaits demolition in July 1965.

When the Rains Came

Nuneaton lying in the Trent valley was often prone to flooding in its town centre.

First photographs of the town under water were taken in 1900 when a newspaper reported: "The whole business quarter of the town was, in a few minutes, turned into a raging torrent when thousands of pounds' worth of damage was caused.

"A remarkable fact was that at about 7am no flooding of the centre of our town was apparent.

"Suddenly the waters swept down and in less than an hour the Market Place and adjacent areas were one huge lake."

But it was the great thunderstorm of May 22, 1932, when the town suffered most damage. The whole central area was plunged underwater bringing chaos as the wooden blocks, which made up the road surface, became a mass of floating debris as the floodwater reached waist high.

The town's elders promised: "We will do something to stop these floods."

But it was several decades – and many more floods – before action was finally taken with the construction of a flood relief channel in the 1970s, stretching from Attleborough to Weddington.

Nuneaton takes to the boats as Market Place and Newdegate Street are swamped by floodwaters in May 1932.

Sailing by – "HMS Nuneaton" floats past the National Provincial Bank.

Paddling time in Market Place.

Staff, believed to be from Nuneaton's Post Office, survey the damage to their sorting offices.

Shop assistants at Lester's Chemist knee-deep in debris.

Lower Abbey Street awash after a torrential downpour.

One horsepower as a family beat the floods.

Showing a leg in Dugdale Street.

All washed up – the Board Inn in Nuneaton's town centre.

Stranded and abandoned – a van in Market Place is surrounded by wooden blocks pushed up from the road surface by the rains. The block roadway had been laid only a few weeks previously.

Beer barrels float down Attleborough Road after the May deluge. This picture was taken from the top of the railway bridge.

Work is halted on the building of Nuneaton's new Council House in Coton Road.

The floods of July 1958, when Nuneaton was hit by a torrential thunderstorm as Bond Gate is closed to traffic.

Church Street, Nuneaton, under several inches of water.

An enterprising canoeist takes to paddle power as he negotiates his way through Mill Walk, Nuneaton, in 1958. The flour mill is in the background.

You can take a horse to water – flood in December 1964.

Traffic negotiates its way through a flooded Bond Gate in June 1968.

Park of Beauty

One of Nuneaton's greatest benefactors was Edward Melly, one of Warwickshire's most powerful coal-mine owners.

Among his lasting gifts to the town is the beautiful Riversley Park, which has been enjoyed by generations for years.

Born in Liverpool in 1857, Mr Melly came to Nuneaton at the age of 25 after being educated at Rugby School and he took over Griff Colliery on the death of Charles Newdegate in 1887.

He was prominent in the public life of Nuneaton, being mayor from 1908 to 1910 and again in 1926-27.

He served as a Justice of the Peace for 40 years and was president of both Nuneaton Rugby Football Club and Nuneaton Amateur Operatic Society.

Riversley Park takes its name from the original Melly family home which overlooked the River Mersey in Liverpool.

Alderman Melly and his wife died in the great air raid of 1941. He lived in Church Street in the house made famous as the "home" of George Eliot's Lawyer Dempster. It is said that the couple refused to move to the cellar when the air-raid siren sounded. Their house received a direct hit.

Benefactor Alderman Edward Melly, who became a Freeman of Nuneaton in 1930, and gave Riversley Park to Nuneaton.

Alderman Melly addresses a large crowd from the bandstand as he presents Riversley Park to the people of Nuneaton in 1907.

Riversley Park in the early part of the century.

Boating on the River Anker in the park in 1980.

Trees and the bandstand silhouetted against the winter sky in 1984.

Another tree for Riversley Park – Nuneaton's jewel in the crown in the annual Britain in Bloom competition. This was planted by Viscountess Daventry (left) to mark the 25th anniversary of Nuneaton Flower Guild in November 1988.

Nuneaton at War

May 17, 1941, is a date that will forever be etched in the history of Nuneaton.

It was the night when it rained death as the might of Hitler's Luftwaffe unleashed a fearsome attack on the town.

One hundred people were killed and many more injured as much of Nuneaton's skyline was flattened and its community ripped apart.

The town was turned into a blazing inferno with churches, homes, shops, factories and air-raid shelters falling victim to the German bombers.

The early part of the raid focused on the Gipsy Lane area, near the Sterling Metals works, where wheels were manufactured for British night-fighters.

Then a woodyard and store close to Trent Valley Station went up in flames after being hit.

As the night wore on the raid intensified with wave after wave of German bombers unleashing their deadly cargo on the town.

As dawn broke, the extent of the grim and bloody horror was revealed as a temporary mortuary was being set up in the George and Dragon public house.

There had been earlier raids on Nuneaton with the first incendiary bomb falling on farmland at Gipsy Lane on August 25, 1940. There was a heavier raid on October 29, of that year.

But it was on May 17, 1941, when the true horror of war was witnessed by the townsfolk.

On June 25, 1942, Nuneaton was again the target of the Luftwaffe when 18 people died and 42 were injured.

The last recorded bomb to fall on the town was on July 28, 1942 – at the Pingles Fields.

Buller Day in Nuneaton as huge crowds pack Abbey Street. 'The crowd was of enormous proportions. The streets were absolutely choked by a cheering, enthusiastic mass of patriotic humanity. Never before was Nuneaton so filled to overflowing,' wrote Harry Fieldhouse, Editor of the *Tribune*, whose readers subscribed to the fund for the war memorial, which now stands in Coton Road, Nuneaton.

An old man in his twilight years bent over his newspaper in the shadow of the Buller statue in Bond Gate. The monument was unveiled on January 28, 1905, by General Sir Redvers Buller VC, to honour the men of Nuneaton who fought and died in the Boer War (1899-1902). Fourteen years later an even more bloody campaign was to put the world in turmoil: World War One. Six-hundred-and-seventy-five men of the borough paid the ultimate price. In 1939 came another world war – a war that came to Nuneaton from the sky.

July 1918: The Mayor, Councillor H.C.Jones, presents the Freedom of the Borough to Lt Leonard Knox and Cpl William Beesley, two Nuneaton men who won the Victoria Cross in World War One.

September 1939: Men of Wheat Street and Vicarage Street demolish a wall to provide bricks for an air-raid shelter.

Outside Riversley Park clinic sandbags are prepared in readiness for German air raids.

Tin hats and smiles in September 1939 outside the Riversley Park clinic "bunker", christened "The Better 'Ole".

This rare aerial picture of Nuneaton was taken by a Luftwaffe reconnaissance aircraft in October, 1940 – to be studied by the Germans before the devastating raid on the town the following year.

Coton Parish Church, made famous as "Shepperton Church", in George Eliot's *Scenes of Clerical Life*, destroyed by German bombers. Later it was rebuilt by German prisoners-of-war.

Alderman Edward Melly, who gave Riversley Park and the Museum and Art Gallery to the town, died with his wife in their Church Street home in the 1941 air raid. One of the major coal-mine owners in Warwickshire, he ran Griff Colliery, served two terms as Mayor and was a magistrate for 40 years. His home was made famous by George Eliot as the home of "Lawyer Dempster".

Corporation Street, which took a direct hit from the Luftwaffe.

Queens Road – part of which was reduced to rubble.

Homes are flattened in Manor Park Road and Manor Court Road.

A soldier walks past the devastated area in Edward Street and Henry Street.

Fitton Street in ruins.

Heath End Road where homes are destroyed.

The *Tribune* in Vicarage Street was destroyed in the great bombing raid of May 1941.

The rotary press – reduced to a tangled wreckage.

The Linotype and composing area.

Nuneaton's wartime civil defence workers.

Nuneaton police first-aid team at the outbreak of the war.

Viscount Montgomery takes the salute at Nuneaton Council House on his visit to unveil the 1939-45 war memorial.

Every year Nuneaton pays tribute to its war dead at the annual Remembrance Day service.

The Role of Bramcote

Nuneaton has been "home" to all three services since June 4, 1940, when RAF Bramcote was commissioned.

In July of that year the first Polish Squadron, No 300 (Masovian) arrived, followed closely by three others, Nos 301, 304 and 305. When they completed their initial training the squadrons left for RAF Swinderby and the station then became headquarters of No 18 Operational Training Unit, whose function was to train aircrew to feed the four other bomber squadrons.

The first aircraft with which the squadrons were equipped were the dive-bombing Fairey Battles, but it was not long before they were replaced with the Wellington and Ansons.

As the war continued 18 OTU was superseded by 105 OTU whose purpose was to train pilots for transport duties, involving a far greater degree of long-distance flying and the use of up-to-date navigational aids. Just before the end of the war Dakotas took over from the Wellingtons, before the handing over to the Royal Navy on December 3, 1946.

The Naval Commanding Officer, in his first address to his crew, called Bramcote the "stone frigate", and reckoned that the White Ensign was being flown in England as far as it was possible to get away from the sea. The ship was named *HMS Gamecock* and its task was to train naval aircraft mechanics.

It was also the home of, at first, 1833 RNVR (Air) Squadron, the weekend flyers with Seafires and eventually Sea Furies, and later 1844 RNVR Squadron with Fireflies. But in March 1957, defence cuts meant all RNVR (Air) Squadrons were disbanded. By then 1,833 had been equipped with jet attackers and had to leave Bramcote because its grass runways were easily burned up.

In April 1959 the Junior Leaders' Regiment Artillery took over, training young men for the Army.

The regiment became involved in the life of Nuneaton building up many strong ties and in 1971 it was granted the Freedom of the Borough.

A formal parade and ceremony was held in May 1972 when the regiment exercised its right to march through the streets of the town "with bayonets fixed and drums beating".

It exercised that right again on June 2, 1990, to mark the 50th anniversary of Bramcote as an operational base.

Bramcote is now home to the 30th Field Regiment of the Royal Signals.

King George VI with wartime leader General Vladislav Sikorski, Prime Minister of the Polish government in exile, inspects a parade at Bramcote shortly after it became a base for Polish squadrons in 1940. General Sikorski was to die two years later in an aircraft accident in Gibraltar.

One of the mascots that was adopted by a Polish squadron at Bramcote during the war.

Polish airmen at Bramcote shortly before joining bomber squadrons at RAF Swinderby are addressed by General Sikorski.

God, Honour and Country – Polish freedom fighters based at Bramcote with the standard of their country's air force, woven by women in occupied Poland and smuggled to England.

May 21, 1972: The Junior Leaders' Regiment Royal Artillery – new Freemen of the Borough – exercise their right to march through the streets of Nuneaton "with bayonets fixed and drums beating".

Town clerk Mr Peter Eccles reads the citation granting the Freedom of the Borough to the Bramcote-based Junior Leaders' Regiment RA watched by officers and the Mayor of Nuneaton, Jimmy James.

The Junior Leaders' Regimental Band pictured before flying to Dortmund in Germany in 1984 when they played in front of the Queen.

A familiar sight in Nuneaton seen during carnivals and parades over many years – the Junior Leaders' Regimental Band in full dress uniform.

It's hats away, we're in the Army now! An annual spectacle at Bramcote Barracks at the end of the annual Goschen passing out parade, marking the end of the Junior Leaders' training period and their progress into the main service.

Commanding Officer Col Isaac (right) and Regimental Brigadier Howarth receive replicas of Victoria Cross citations presented to Nuneaton's two World War One heroes, Lt Leonard Knox and Cpl William Beesley. The presentation was made by the Mayor George Taylor.

A Town at Work

Although the coal industry was the main source of employment for the people of Nuneaton, quarrying, the hosiery industry and engineering all played an important role in the life of the town.

But now names like Listers, Slingsbys, Fielding and Johnson, Sterling Metals and Courtaulds are just memories.

New industries have been attracted to the town but are less labour-intensive.

Part of Nuneaton's mineral wealth – the William Boon quarry at Windmill Hill photographed in 1906.

Making machinery for the coal-mining industry, workers at Nuneaton Engineering Company at their Tuttle Hill foundry in the early 1900s.

An early twentieth-century picture of workmen at Judkins quarry, Nuneaton, where the freehold rights were bought in 1864 for £5,000.

The early years of Galliford. Thomas Galliford, company founder, beside the rear wheel of a steamroller with men of the road-mending team. The horse-drawn water carrier alongside was an essential part of the gang.

At full stretch – Courtaulds Mill in Marlborough Road which was once Nuneaton's biggest employer. Now it is a site for a new housing development.

Women workers at Listers, Nuneaton, in the 1950s.

Inside the box manufacturer's factory of Alfred Conner in Fife Street, Nuneaton, pictured in March 1951.

Another landmark that has disappeared from the Nuneaton skyline – the flour mill which stood in Mill Walk and was built in 1886.

King Coal of Nuneaton

Nuneaton was founded on a wealth of coal, clay and stone, with old records showing that as long ago as 1275 a man by the name of Alexander Compton was granted a licence to mine "black gold" at Coton.

It was King Coal who reigned supreme with the town rightly acclaiming to be the capital of the Warwickshire Coalfield.

Nuneaton miners could be found working at any one of the 20-odd pits that was in travelling distance of their homes.

In the mid-1950s, one fifth of the working male population was employed in the mining industry.

But as reserves ran out, names such as Griff No 4, Griff Clara, Haunchwood (The Tunnel), Ansley Hall and Arley passed into the pages of history.

Only those who have been down into the bowels of the earth know how tough coal mining can be. It was hard, thirsty and dangerous work with many a pitman losing his life.

One such tragedy happened at Newdigate Colliery (1894-1982) on September 3, 1931, when eight men lost their lives following an explosion.

It was customary after such tragedies for poem sheets to be sold to raise money for the dependents of the victims.

One verse of the poem written after the Newdigate explosion reads:

Rescuers tried their utmost
And worked themselves out of breath,
But the dark angel had flown through the pit
Leaving its toll of death.

The sinking of Newdigate Colliery in 1898.

The Tunnel pit (Haunchwood) as it was in 1965. Now the slag heaps no longer dominate the skyline.

Arley Colliery tip being levelled in November 1966.

All smiles from under the ground at Newdigate Colliery – but soon it was to be announced that the pit would close.

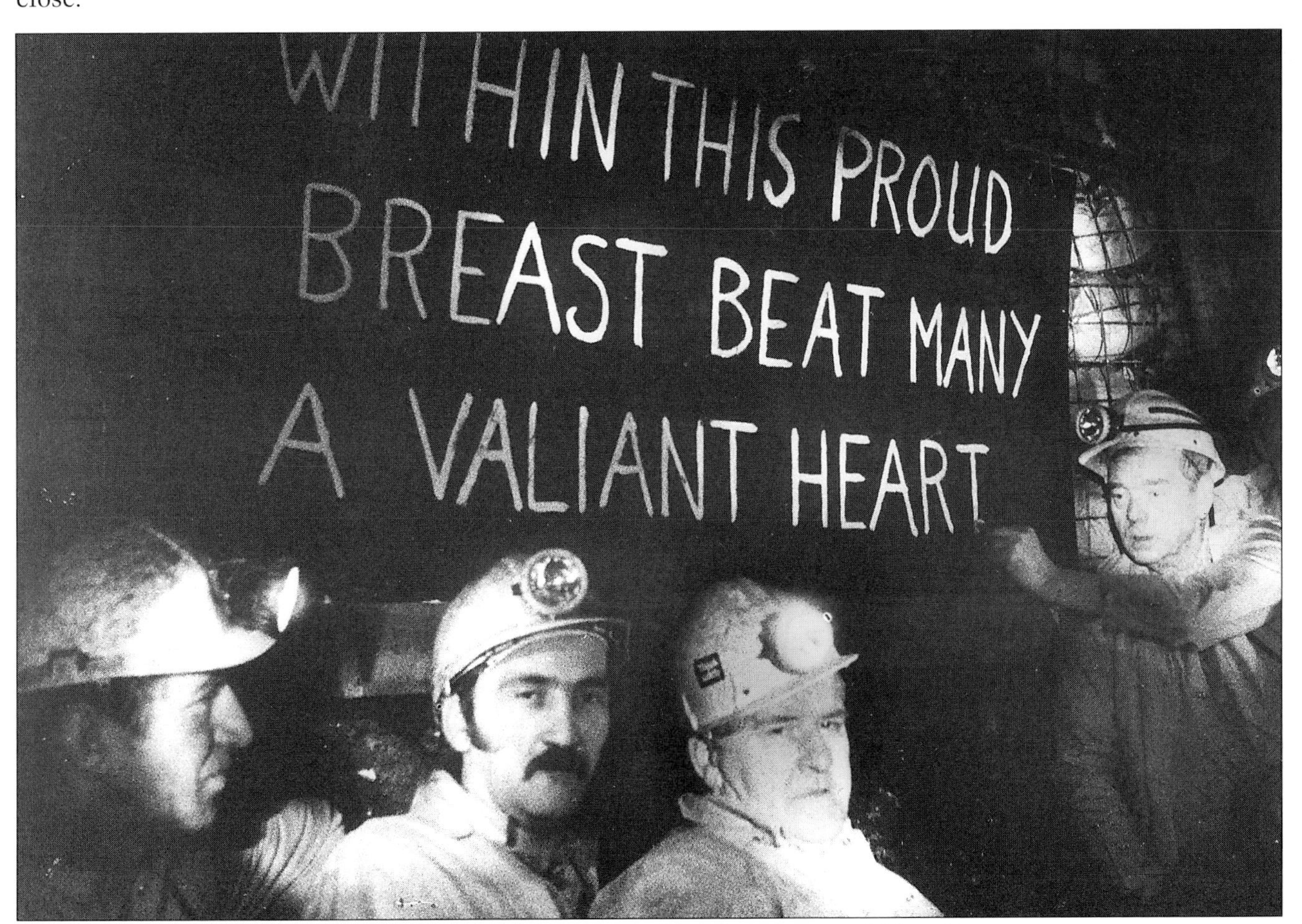

March 1982: One of the last messages left underground by the pitmen of Newdigate.

Jobs were to be transferred and it was the end of an era at Newdigate in 1982, but the miners could still share a joke as they leave the pit bottom for the last time.

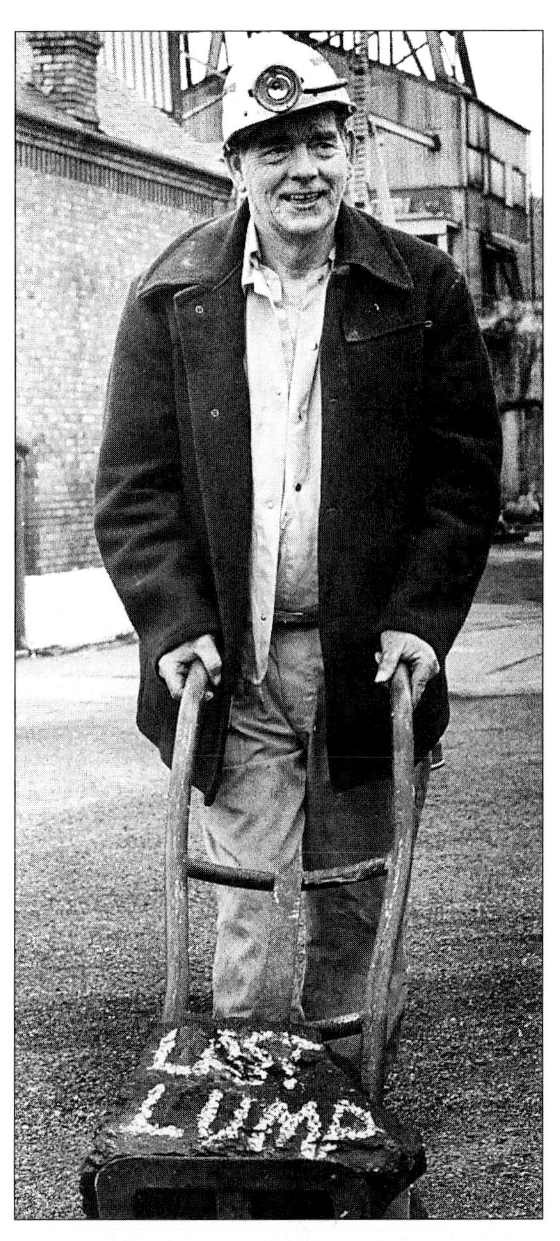

Newdigate training officer Albert Cox with the last lump of coal brought up from Newdigate Colliery.

Made redundant – a pit canary loses its job at Newdigate Colliery.

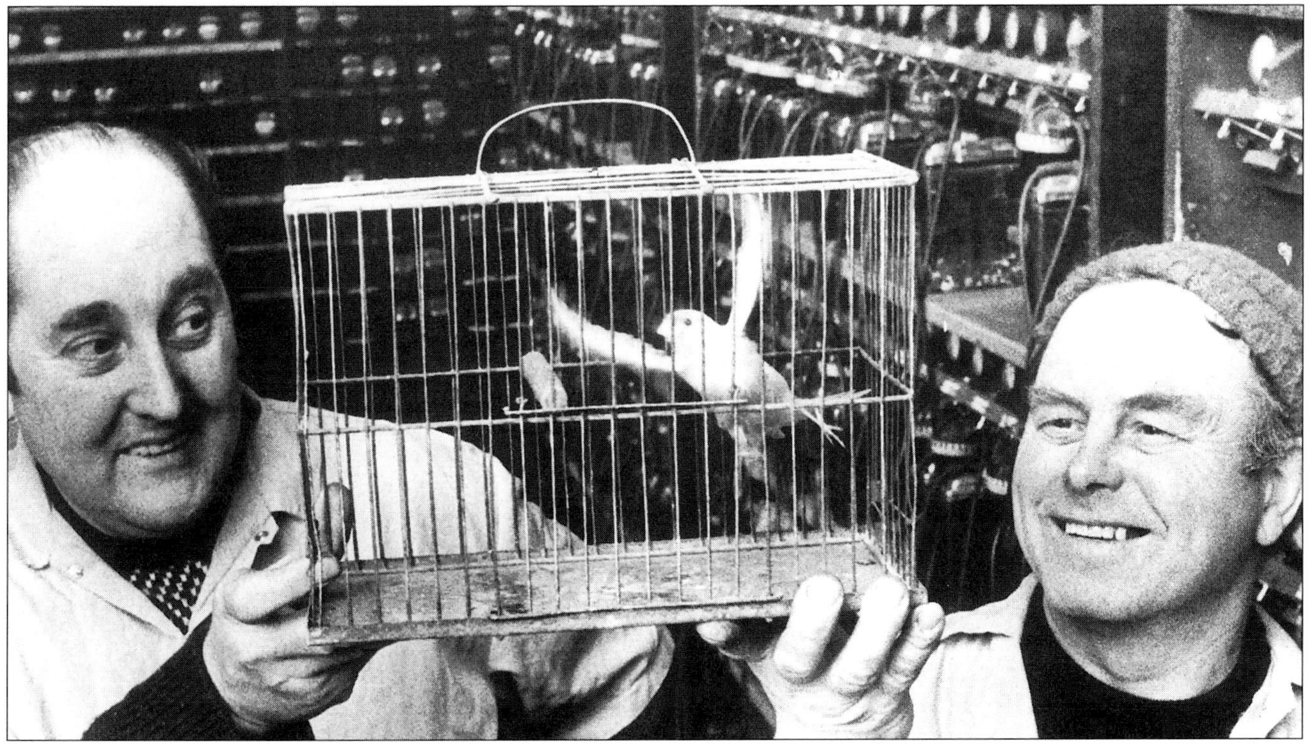

Baddesley Pit at Baxterley, which ceased production in 1989 after turning coal for 139 years.

Keresley Colliery, which in its heyday employed more than 1,300 miners, closed by British Coal – but later re-opened under private ownership and named Coventry Mine.

Striking miners outside Daw Mill Colliery during the bitter miners' strike of 1984. The pit's work-force was divided during the dispute with many men joining the UDM.

Keresley Homefire Plant in 1983.

National Union of Mineworkers' members on picket duty outside Keresley Colliery in March 1984.

NUM leader Arthur Scargill addresses miners at Nicholas Chamberlaine School in a bid to gain more support for the crippling strike.

On the march in April 1984: Demonstrators join Nuneaton Trades Council members as they walk through Coton Arches, Nuneaton, to Bedworth, in support of the miners.

No confrontation: A policeman joins striking miners around a makeshift fire outside Daw Mill Colliery.

Bearing gifts from abroad: Parcels of clothing and toys arrive in January 1985 from West German trade unionists for striking Warwickshire miners.

The Sad Times

Although the bombing raids in World War Two were undoubtedly the most tragic times for Nuneaton, the town has suffered other tragedies over the years.

In 1924 there was an horrendous bus fire on the Cock and Bear bridge when seven people lost their lives.

And on New Year's Day 1966, the town was in mourning after four people lost their lives at a New Year's Eve Dance at the town's mecca for youngsters – the Co-operative Hall. They were killed in a crush as revellers made their way down the stairs to the dance floor to welcome in the New Year with *Auld Lang Syne*.

The biggest peacetime fire seen in Nuneaton, in December 1967, luckily did not claim any lives.

But it was a spectacular sight when the giant Awson Carriageworks factory in Meadow Street was ablaze with the flames clearly visible many miles away. The fire was so fierce and extensive that firemen from all over the county had to be drafted in to fight the flames.

It was on a hot summer's night on June 6, 1975, that tragedy was again to strike the town.

The night sleeper express from Euston to Glasgow was running late and at 1.55am was heading towards Nuneaton Trent Valley Station where a temporary speed limit had been imposed during railtrack repairs.

The train failed to slow down and crashed into the station, killing six passengers and injuring many more.

In Nuneaton's biggest peacetime rescue operation, firemen, police, ambulancemen, doctors and nurses battled through the tangled wreckage to reach the victims.

It is a night that will be long remembered in the town.

December 1967: Like a monster from another world, the stark skeleton of Awson Carriageworks is silhouetted against the night sky.

Firemen battle in vain to contain the flames at the Awson Carriageworks factory blaze.

Two sombre-faced police constables on duty outside Nuneaton Co-operative Hall on New Year's Day 1966. The night before revellers had been welcoming in the New Year when tragedy struck and four people died when they were crushed on the stairs of the dance hall.

June 1975: Minutes after the Euston sleeper left the rails, rescuers reach the scene to find total carnage.

Battling throughout the night to reach the victims.

A victim is pulled alive from the crashed train after rescuers spent several hours cutting him free.

Firemen on top of a wrecked sleeper coach cut their way through to the compartments.

A welcome cup of tea for weary rescuers. Within a short space of time Mrs Paulette Jones, district organiser of the Women's Royal Voluntary Service, assembled a team of helpers. They set up an emergency station at the nearby old people's centre in Newtown Road serving hot cups of tea to dazed passengers and a trackside refreshment tea bar for the rescuers, who because of the searing heat could only work in short shifts.

A call for silence – firemen listen for for signs of life, not knowing how many people are still trapped.

Nuneaton train driver Ramesh Patel was sitting in the cab of his goods train when the windscreen was shattered by flying debris from the crash. "I think it is a miracle I am alive," he said, as he surveyed the extent of the damage at Trent Valley Station.

A gantry which was brought crashing to the ground proved an extra hazard for rescuers.

In the cold light of day, Nuneaton MP Leslie Huckfield (foreground left) and Chief Inspector Wesley Watkins survey the crash scene as rescuers continue their search for victims.

An aerial scene of the crash, taken the next day as hundreds of onlookers witness the extent of the tragedy.

Nuneaton at Play

Entertainment in Victorian times was often provided at "Till's Yard", in Abbey Street, an open space of land on which the Liberal Club was later built.

Portable theatre companies would visit the town performing plays with the travelling actors parading in the streets blowing a trumpet and banging a drum as a way of advertising their next performance.

In 1889, Edward Arnold Shute founded Nuneaton Dramatic Society with its first production R.E.Francillon's *Old Father Time* being staged on November 11 at the old Drill Hall in Mill Walk.

It was a charity performance in aid of Nuneaton Fire Brigade with tickets priced at one shilling for a front seat and sixpence for others.

For the next six years annual productions took place at the Drill Hall, but on July 21, 1895 there was a new venue when Nuneaton's Theatre Royal was opened in New Bridge Street.

What was to become Nuneaton's main centre of entertainment for half a century, the Prince of Wales Theatre, was opened in 1900, a grand building with an ornate façade. (It closed in 1956 and was destroyed by fire on June 22, 1968).

It was later renamed the Hippodrome and became a cinema and in the 1930s was one of six in the town centre along with the Royal, the Palace, the Princes and the Ritz and Scala, buildings which still stand today, but are no longer used to show films. Attleborough, Stockingford and Chapel End, too, could boast their own picture houses.

Moving pictures, however, did not destroy live theatre in Nuneaton with the town's Operatic and Dramatic Society being founded in 1920.

It has staged shows every year since, with the exception of 1940-47.

Nuneaton's Pantomime Society each year puts on a show, but now, sadly, like NAODS, performances have to be staged out of town at the Civic Hall in neighbouring Bedworth because Nuneaton no longer has a suitable venue.

Edward Arnold Shute, who founded Nuneaton Dramatic Society in 1889.

The Prince of Wales Theatre (Hippodrome) opened in Bond Gate in 1900 and for half a century, the town's main centre of entertainment. It closed in 1956 and 12 years later was destroyed by fire.

Nuneaton Operatic Society on stage of the Prince of Wales Theatre in May 1909.

Cast of Nuneaton Operatic and Dramatic Society in one of their earliest productions of the *Mikado*, staged in 1926.

Marjorie Clarke, who took the title role in "Miss Hook of Holland", in 1927.

The Scala Theatre in Abbey Street in the early 1950s, once one of six cinemas in Nuneaton town centre.

Two stalwarts of Nuneaton Amateur Operatic Society – producer and musical director Aubrey Allen and Madam Bertha Sharrod, for many years the accompanist, pictured in the 1950s.

The dancing girls who took part in NAODS's performance of *Rose Marie* at the Hippodrome Theatre in 1952. Left to right: Gladys Powell, Myra Chadaway, Margaret Dewis, Mollie Kendall, Vicky Booker, Jean Wykes, Nancy Bates, Brenda Grant, Mavis Hall, Eileen Hughes, Valerie Collier, Barbara Evans, Margaret Collier, Shirley Paul and Cynthia Horne.

Unbeknown to the cast, Nuneaton's King of Comedy Larry Grayson was in the audience watching Nuneaton Pantomime Society's 1980 production of *Robinson Crusoe* at the Ritz Cinema and at the end went on the stage to say: "What a gay play!"

The gentlemen chorus and children in the Pantomime Society's *Pied Piper of Hamelin* in 1981.

Chorus girls in the *Pied Piper*.

Jeff Little and Margaret Hollis in the 1984 pantomime *Ali Baba and the Forty Thieves*.

Members of Nuneaton Pantomime Society present a theatre mask for the borough's civic silver collection to Mayor Albert Walker in 1986.

Carnival and Party Time

Carnival time in Nuneaton has been a tradition dating back to 1930 when revellers first took to the streets to raise money for the General Hospital.

Over the years thousands of pounds have been raised for local charities from the colourful procession of floats and bands parading through the town.

The carnival is the biggest fun-day of the year, always attracting large crowds.

But in 1986 an even bigger fun-day took place when the first Victorian Christmas evening was held. Local shops, together with the Borough Council and supported by the *Tribune*, organised a November night of late shopping with a feast of street entertainment.

No one knew how many people would come and see the switching on of the Christmas lights.

In the event, an estimated 30,000 people crammed into the town centre – the biggest crowd seen in Nuneaton since the announcement of the end of World War Two.

Far left: Ann Seal, Nuneaton's first Carnival Queen, crowned in 1930.
Left: Phyllis Gibbs, who became Carnival Queen in 1931.

Staff of Nuneaton sports specialists F.H.Ayres Limited prepare to take part in the 1931 carnival procession.

Carnival Queen Mary Haynes with her maids of honour, Phyllis Gibbs, Dorothy Widdus, Vera Cox, Iris Barratt and Fannie Timmins in 1932.

Vera Phillips of Galley Common being crowned Carnival Queen in Riversley Park in 1938 by the Mayor, Ald W.Croshaw.

Nuneaton's King of Mirth, K.Jepson, collects money for charity at the 1938 carnival.

The Black and White Minstrels on parade in 1963.

Child walkers in the 1963 carnival.

Young at heart – members of the Over Sixties Club.

Adults and children on parade in 1963.

Nuneaton Parks Department girls with the carnival message: Cultivate tidiness.

Stockingford AA's "Stone Age" entry in the 1967 carnival.

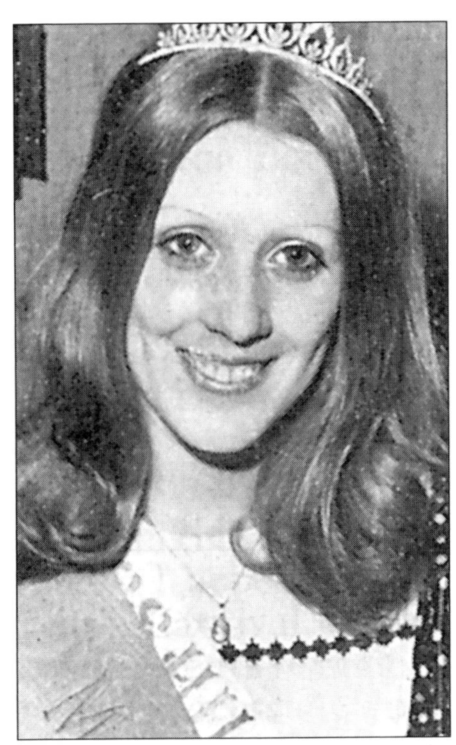

Vicki Deeming, Nuneaton's 1973 Carnival Queen; Sheila Wright and Denise Kearns, the 1973 maids of honour.

Nuneaton King of Mirth and his Merry Men. Back row: Roger Fox, Bob Warmington, Andy Johnson. Centre left: Graham Bennett. Front: David Gibbons, Gef White and David Adney.

November 1986: Nuneaton's first Victorian late night shopping party when an estimated 30,000 people crammed into the town centre.

Nuneaton police chief Supt Frank Garrett as a Victorian policeman (left) dresses for the occasion at Nuneaton's 1986 Victorian Night.

The late Cec Burton joins helpers at the League of Friends stall in 1986.

Carol singing at Nuneaton's first Victorian night.

The lights go on for the start of the 1989 Victorian celebrations.

Girls from Marks and Spencer light up the night.

O Come All Ye Faithful... members of Bedworth Amateur Show Society entertain with carols at the main Abbey Street Co-op store.

Right: Trevor Ashby hits the high note for charity.

Far right: Royal visit to the *Tribune* – Queen Victoria and the Prince of Wales (alias Alice and George de Mellet de Bonas) at the newspaper's former printing house in Whitacre Road.

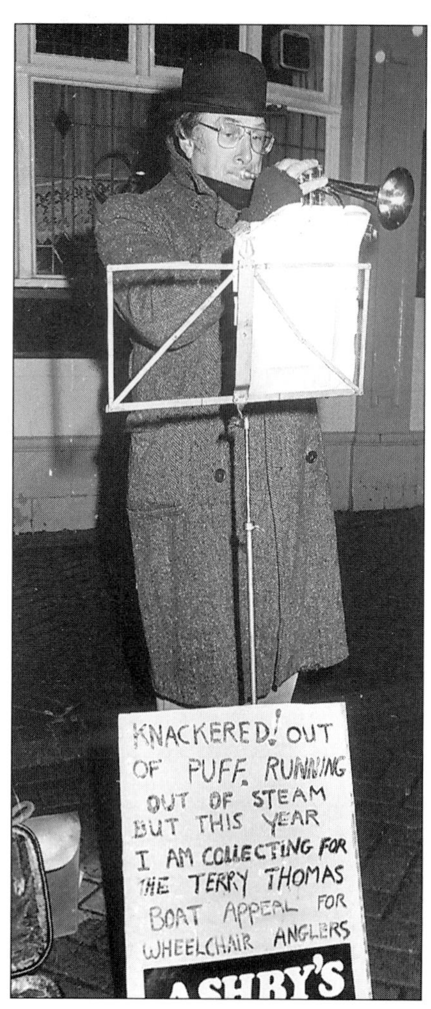

Victorian costume ball held in 1989 at St George's Hall.

The golden age of Queen Victoria at the East Mercia Co-op in 1989.

Nuneaton's King of Comedy

A young lad stood on Trent Valley Railway Station, waiting to be collected by his new foster parents, a miner's family from Abbey Green.

He had been born to an unmarried woman in Banbury, but came to regard Nuneaton as his home town.

Nearly 50 years later he was to put it on the map, making it known to millions of television viewers.

Schoolboy William Sully-White became entertainer Larry Grayson. After years of touring the local clubs as Billy Breen he was rocketed to stardom.

In 1972 he had his own TV show, named after his catch-phrase *Shut That Door*, topped the bill at the London Palladium, appeared in front of royalty, was chosen as Showbiz Personality of the Year and featured in *This is Your Life*.

Larry went on to host the nation's number-one television programme, *The Generation Game* – watched by a 16-million strong audience every Saturday night.

But despite the fame, "Our Bill" remained loyal to his Nuneaton roots.

After going into semi-retirement, he lived modestly, in a small bungalow near the town centre.

It was there he died suddenly, in January 1995, aged 71, after undergoing an appendix operation.

Larry on the set of his TV show *Shut That Door*.

Cutting the tape to open the Intensive Care Unit at George Eliot Hospital. To Larry's right are former Mayor George Taylor and former Warwickshire County Council Chairman Jack Brindley.

Walking his poodle Peter in Clifton Road, where he lived when fame came knocking at his door.

Generation Game fun, with co-host Isla St Clair.

Being entertained by catering students at North Warwickshire College.

On horseback at the Galley Common Riding School for the Disabled, alongside ex-Mayor Harold Jones.

With his devoted sister Fan, at Everard Road – the name of one of Larry's fictitious characters.

Sporting Nuneaton

Nuneaton is a town with a fine tradition for sport.

Nuneaton Cricket Club has the distinction of being the oldest sports club in the borough and in the 1870s fielded cricket, soccer and rugby teams.

Ten years later Nuneaton St Nicolas FC was formed, which was the forerunner of Nuneaton Town, started in 1890.

The club went out of existence in 1937 and became Nuneaton Boro' – a club that graduated from the old Birmingham League into the Southern League and were founder members of the non-League's élite Alliance Premier League.

Problems off the field almost led to the Boro's downfall in the late 1980s but the club was re-formed by a group of local businessmen.

Over the years the Boro' have been renowned for their exploits in the FA Cup. In 1966-67 they reached the third round, going out in a replay at Rotherham after beating Swansea. The two gates at Manor Park, against Swansea and Rotherham, attracted a total of 40,000 fans.

In 1993 Boro' again beat Swansea to reach the second round. They drew at Bournemouth, only to lose 1-0 in a home replay that drew a 4,000 attendance and was screened live on Sky TV.

Nuneaton Rugby Club, which celebrated its centenary in the 1979-80 season, plays many of the country's top clubs. Its home in Attleborough Road was sold in 1994 for housing development with the club moving to a new ground off Eastboro' Way ring road.

Nuneaton Town Football Club in the 1897-98 season.

Nuneaton United FC at the start of the 1920-21 season.

An unusual picture of the town's football team in 1934-35.

Nuneaton has always sported a number of fine amateur soccer sides. This is Stockingford Old Scholars in 1947.

Nuneaton Old Edwardians rugby team, 1951-52. Back row (left to right): Barry Gould, Harry Fitton, Frank Bazeley, Desmond Chaplin, Cliff Dickenson, Laurence Bloxham, Terry Savage, Norman Worrall, Donald Wheway, Jack Betteridge (trainer), Robert Bennett. Front row: Frank Moore, Alec Hill, Sid Gregory, Bob Arnold, Ray Bayliss, Keith Wilson and Brian Cooke.

Fred Badham, the Nuneaton Boro' boss, gives an early season pep-talk to the Manor Park ball boys in September 1966 as he develops a youth policy for Nuneaton youngsters.

January 1967: A huge poster outside Manor Park football ground advertising the match against Swansea Town, which the Boro' won to earn a home tie against Rotherham.

One of Boro's best sides, the 1985 team, which finished runners-up in the Alliance. Four players – Richard Hill, Paul Culpin, Trevor Morley and Eddie McGoldrick – went on to play in the First Division. The side, managed by Graham Carr, was: Back (left to right) Everton Carr, Brendan Phillips, Ian Bennyworth, Richard Dixey, Alan Poole, Richard Hill, Timmy Smithers, Willie Gibson, Dave Looms (trainer). Front: Frank Murphy, Stuart Hamill, Paul Culpin, Trevor Morley, Eddie McGoldrick and Mick Thurman.

Cup joy: Boro' players celebrate after their 1993 FA Cup win against Swansea.

Nuneaton RFC in 1991. Back row (left to right): Alan Taylor, John Cannon, Guy Hawthorn, Dom Mellor, Steve Carter, John Gardner, Rob Milner, Mark Gardner, Charlie Evans. Front row: Paul Jones, Simon Jarvis, Tom Temple, Darren Barry, Alphonso Cain, Gareth Mitchell and Chris Churm.

Bonjour Nuneaton!

The hands of friendship have bridged the English Channel since the mid-1950s when Nuneaton and the French town of Roanne on the River Loire became "twinned".

Thousands of schoolchildren, firemen, policemen, hospital staff, Rotarians, clergymen, cultural societies and others have exchanged visits as the two towns built a foundation, cemented before the Treaty of Rome and the Common Market.

Roanne Ringway in Nuneaton and Rue Nuneaton in Roanne are roads named after the twins. And the two local authorities have, over the years, bonded a family relationship between the towns which shows no sign of weakening.

Welcome to Nuneaton: Mayor Sam Walters welcomes his Roanne counterpart at Trent Valley station when a French delegation paid an exchange visit to the town in 1969. Also in the picture are Town Clerk and Solicitor Peter Eccles (second left) and Alderman Reg Hadden (third left).

The Mayor of Nuneaton and Bedworth Terry Short hosts a civic reception for Roanne visitors in October 1979.

Bill Deacon welcomes Roanne schoolchildren to the mayor's parlour in July 1980.

Roanne firemen during a visit to Nuneaton fire station in May 1980.

The hand of friendship from Mayor Jeff Place when Roanne Rugby Football Club were guests in Nuneaton in September 1981.

Have bike will travel – French cyclists visiting Mayor John Haynes at Nuneaton Council House in May 1982.

Have bike will travel back – Nuneaton firemen in April 1984 prepare their route for a marathon cycle ride to France. Left to right: David Perry, Bob Jenkins, Derek Harwood, Barry Haywood, Terry Owen and Stephen Manning.

Saying it with flowers – a floral display in Bedworth Miners' Welfare Park welcomes French visitors to the borough, celebrating the 25th anniversary of the twinning with Roanne in 1981.

Mayor Mrs Kit Ward welcomes M. S.Feugere, Roanne's Principal Deputy Mayor in September 1982.

Mayor Stan Williams (right) and Deputy Mayor Albert Walker in 1984 with candelabra, a gift from Roanne which is now part of Nuneaton's civic silver collection.

It's good to see you again. All smiles as Marie-Laure Laine (left) from Roanne is welcomed to the town by her Nuneaton 'twin' Rachel Hinds.

A commemorative stone is unveiled in Riversley Park to mark the 25th anniversary of twinning link between Nuneaton and Roanne.

Arise Sir William – Roanne vintner Paul-Louis Lapandery confers the ancient winegrowers' knighthood on Mayor Bill Olner, who became a member of the Order of the Old Wine Press (*Vieux Pressoir*).

Royal Nuneaton

There have been a number of royal visits to Nuneaton over the years. In 1924 King George VI, then the Duke of York, opened the miners' convalescent home at Higham-on-the-Hill.

His mother, the redoubtable Queen Mary, came to Arbury Hall in the summer of 1927, but there was little publicity.

On July 10, 1934, the Prince of Wales, later to become the Duke of Windsor, paid a flying visit. His aircraft landed in a field at Caldecote and large crowds gathered in Weddington Road to cheer him on his way to a civic reception at Nuneaton Council House.

He went to Swinnerton School, Hall and Phillips hat factory and Manor Hospital before lunching at Arbury Hall with Sir Francis and Lady Newdegate.

On August 20, 1940, King George VI and Queen Elizabeth paid a top-secret visit to RAF Bramcote to inspect a squadron of Polish airmen.

Two years later, on February 25, 1942, the King and Queen returned to Nuneaton, to inspect its civil defence forces, watched by thousands of people.

One of Britain's favourite royals, Princess Alexandra, was in town on February 2, 1968, to open Sunnyside Court housing development, off Croft Road, and later the new Maternity Hospital.

Crowds turned out in their hundreds when Princess Anne came to Nuneaton on March 20, 1985, to visit Abbey Hosiery Mills and the Intec YTC centre. She was back in town four years later visiting Adams Childrenswear at Attleborough Fields and the nearby Centenary Business Centre.

A third visit of the Princess Royal came on January 14, 1991, at the official opening of the Mary Ann Evans Hospice. Much of the money for the hospice had been raised by public subscription.

Nuneaton's biggest royal day came on December 8, 1994, when Queen Elizabeth and Prince Philip were welcomed by huge crowds.

They were in the town to visit Higham Lane School where students showed her a calf from the royal herd which they had acquired for their rural studies farm.

King George V decorates Nuneaton VC hero Lt Leonard Knox during World War One.

The royal couple then went to George Eliot Hospital to open officially the multi-million pound Phase III development.

The Prince of Wales, later the Duke of Windsor, at Swinnerton School in July 1934.

The Prince of Wales watches hat production at Hall and Phillips hat factory in Meadow Street, Nuneaton.

On a wet December day in 1936, crowds gather outside Nuneaton Council House to hear the Proclamation, read by the Mayor, Alderman T.L.Liggins, of the accession of King George VI.

The flags are out in Bridge Street in May 1937, to mark the Coronation of King George VI.

Civic celebrations outside a decorated Council House for King George VI's Coronation.

King George VI inspects Nuneaton's Civil Defence Corps in Coton Road on February 25, 1942.

Women Civil Defence workers on royal parade in 1942.

King George VI and Queen Elizabeth's civic wartime welcome to Nuneaton.

The Coton Road entrance to Riversley Park, decorated for the Coronation of Queen Elizabeth II in June 1953.

A family celebrates the 1953 Coronation at a street party in Arlon Avenue, Nuneaton.

Princess Anne at Nuneaton Training Service's Intec centre in Whitacre Road in 1985.

Swinnerton schoolchildren raise a cheer for Princess Anne in 1985.

Crowds line the streets during Princess Anne's visit to Abbey Hosiery.

Royal walkabout during Princess Anne's 1989 visit to Nuneaton.

The Princess Royal unveils a commemorative window at the Mary Ann Evans Hospice in January 1991.

A royal chat at Nuneaton Hospice at its official opening.

Down on the farm: The Queen talks to teacher John Terry and students Oliver Merson, Lee Soames and Ben Lloyd with Higham Lane School's prizewinning Kerry Blue sheep.

The Queen at Higham Lane School farm sees one of her calves from the royal herd.

Cheers for the Queen and Prince Philip from crowds in Shanklin Drive, Nuneaton, during the visit in December 1994.

A fitting welcome from Higham Lane languages students.

Prince Philip talks to Higham Lane students.

The Queen signs the visitors' book during her visit to mark the completion of the multi-million pound Phase III development at George Eliot Hospital.

The Queen comes face to face with herself after unveiling a bronze bust by Nuneaton sculptor John Letts (left).

Prince Philip is introduced to Nuneaton MP Bill Olner at George Eliot Hospital.

Meeting the staff at Nuneaton's new-look hospital.

Political Pendulum

Nuneaton's political pendulum has swung to and fro over the years. The Centre, Right and Left have all enjoyed their victories as Liberals, Tories and Labour have returned Members of Parliament to represent the constituency.

Post-war politics in Nuneaton saw Frank Bowles as its Labour MP, who was first elected in a 1942 by-election. A solicitor by profession, he held the seat until 1964 when he was elevated to the House of Lords to make way for Frank Cousins, the General Secretary of the Transport and General Workers' Union, seeking an ultra-safe seat.

Cousins became the Minister of Technology in Wilson's Cabinet but resigned two years later.

His resignation became the springboard for one of Nuneaton's most flamboyant MPs, Leslie Huckfield, who was returned in a 1967 by-election with a 4,054 majority. He rose to be a Junior Industry Minister and an Opposition Front Bench Spokesman, but in 1981, following boundary changes, when the constituency was to lose Bedworth to North Warwickshire, he said he was intending to leave Nuneaton and become the prospective parliamentary candidate for the safe seat of Wigan. His attempt was unsuccessful.

In the 1983 General Election Lew Stevens took the new Nuneaton seat for the Conservatives with a 5,061 majority.

Huckfield went on to become Merseyside's Euro MP between 1984 and 1989.

Stevens lost his seat to former Labour Mayor Bill Olner in April 1992.

General Election nomination day, November 4, 1935, on the steps of Nuneaton Council House. Back row: Col F.S.Hanson DSO, H.R.Williams (secretary and agent), Cllr G.C.Teebay. Middle row: Mrs D'Arcy Chaytor, Mrs Moreton, C.E.Neath, Col D'Arcy Chaytor. Third row: Miss A.H.Moreton, Sir Francis Newdegate, Lady Dugdale JP. Front row: John Moores (National Government candidate).

Left: Leslie Huckfield, who became Labour MP for Nuneaton and Bedworth in 1967, was the youngest member of the House at the age of 24. He is pictured at a TUC day-of-action in Nuneaton in 1980.

Below: Lew Stevens (second right) on the campaign trail in 1983 before successfully taking the Nuneaton seat.

Bottom: Bill Olner, as Mayor of Nuneaton and Bedworth in 1988, when he spearheaded a civic appeal campaign to raise money to build the Mary Ann Evans Hospice, pictured with members of Nuneaton Darby and Joan Club. Four years later he became Nuneaton's MP.

Bird's-eye View

One of the earliest bird's-eye pictures of Nuneaton taken in 1900. The running track of the Newdegate Arms sports ground can be seen in the top left-hand corner.

Nuneaton from the air in 1957: Biddles factory, now demolished, in Newtown Road, is easily identified, near the newly constructed bus station.

The town centre before the ring road in 1966. A.J.Pearce's departmental store (the white building, middle left), can be seen close to the Palace Cinema.

A Nuneaton landmark, which has now disappeared – Fielding and Johnson worsted yarn mill, once a cotton mill, off Attleborough Road.

Nuneaton in 1949 showing the Town Hall (then called the Council House) middle right, behind which stood the flour mill.

Henry Street (left), Bridge Street and Coton Arches as they were in August 1963.

George Eliot Maternity Hospital, under construction in April 1966.

St Nicolas Park, Nuneaton's biggest private housing estate from the air, with the village of Higham (top right).

North Warwickshire College, pictured in 1983.

Manor Park, home of Nuneaton Boro' Football Club, in the centre.

St Nicolas Parish Church and (top right) Nuneaton Museum and Art Gallery.

Abbey Green and the town centre with Attleborough at the top.

The familiar landmark at Coton Arches and All Saints' Parish Church.

George Eliot Hospital before its major redevelopment programme.

Looking down on Whitacre Road industrial estate with Nuneaton cemetery (top centre).

Once Nuneaton's major employers, Sterling Metals, before it was demolished to make way for housing development.

Attleborough from the air.

Ancient and Modern

One of Nuneaton's fine buildings which can still be seen today – the old police station and Mining School. This picture was taken in 1900 and shows the weir which ran from Wash Brook.

An ivy clad King Edward VI Grammar School (founded 1552) in the early 1900s.

Before the age of the car – Nuneaton Market Place, *c.*1910.

Nuneaton General Hospital (later the Manor) at the beginning of the century. It closed as a hospital when all its services were transferred to the George Eliot complex in 1993.

Nuneaton's old council offices and fire station in Queens Road.

Nuneaton's Free Library in Coton Road after £2,000 had been raised by public subscription. It was opened in 1898 but later demolished to make way for the new Council House.

Nuneaton's Electric Light Station in 1902.

A 1920s bus negotiates Coventry Road canal bridge, before the road was widened.

The leafy Church Street, Nuneaton, *c.*1925.

Tuttle Hill Windmill in the 1930s, which was often the victim of wind damage! Sails were torn from it in 1906, 1929 and 1936, when just a stump remained.

A picture, believed to have been taken in the early 1950s, looking towards the Market Place. The Bull Hotel (later the George Eliot Hotel), right, was opposite the former main general post office (hidden, left).

Nuneaton Cattle Market in the 1950s, when every week livestock used to be brought into the town. The market stood in Harefield Road, opposite the present site of the bus station.

Abbey Street in the 1950s, shortly after new lighting had been installed.

Making sure Nuneaton has a better water supply. Work in progress on Oldbury Reservoir at Hartshill, in September 1953.

Seeswood Pool in Astley Lane, which dropped to its lowest level in years after the long dry spell of 1959.

Nuneaton Public Library, Church Street, nears completion in 1962. It was designed by Sir Frederick Gibberd, architect of Liverpool Roman Catholic Cathedral.

June 1959: A street market in Nuneaton when it was held only on Saturdays.

BARCL
OFFICES
F.W. WOOLWORTH & Co. LTD
Boots
DISPENSING
Boots

Nuneaton's open swimming pool situated at St Mary's Road, in 1964. It was closed when the new Pingles leisure complex, with an indoor pool, opened in 1965.

Chilvers Coton railway station, pictured on January 17, 1965, shortly before its closure.

Stockingford Station, on the Birmingham to Leicester line, now demolished.

The old Abbey Street Station, where hundreds of people used to commute to Birmingham each day.

Boffins Passage in the 1960s, so called because of the popular shop where cold meat rolls were a speciality.

Coton Road, Nuneaton, at the corner of Princes Street, in July 1963.

Moore's Pot Shop, as it was in Abbey Street, Nuneaton, in 1963.

Church Street, Nuneaton, opposite Bridge Street, in June 1963. In the background (right) is Nuneaton's new police station under construction.

Victoria Street, Nuneaton, in October 1966, looking towards Windsor Street and the Windsor Hotel. The street vanished with the building of Roanne Ringway.

More homes that have disappeared with the building of Nuneaton's ring road – Princes Street, looking towards Coton Road.

Nuneaton centre in upheaval in the 1980s as work is in progress laying block paving in readiness for the pedestrianisation scheme.

April 1985: Shadow Environment Minister John Cunningham MP (third left), inspects the site for Nuneaton's first multi-storey car park at the corner of Newtown Road and Harefield Road. In the background is Biddles factory, which was later demolished.

Workmen erecting new shelters during the refurbishment of Nuneaton central bus station in September 1988.

Faces of the Town

Joseph Henry Pipe, captain of Nuneaton Fire Brigade in the early 1900s, was also landlord of the Railway Tavern in Bond End.

Nuneaton Fire Brigade with its engine and appliances in 1902.

John Bostock, the Nuneaton butcher, with a prize beast, in Bond End in 1900.

Pupils of Heath End School in 1905-06.

Be Prepared: Boys Scouts of the First Nuneaton Troop in 1908.

Manor Park School pupils shortly before the outbreak of World War Two in 1939.

Pupils of Nuneaton High School for Girls, in July 1946.

Edwin Simpson, the *Tribune's* longest-serving journalist, who joined the newspaper shortly after its birth in 1895. He was editor for many years before retiring at the age of 70.

Albert Jebbett, who was responsible for the growth of the *Tribune* in the 1950s and 60s.

Staff of Nuneaton High School for Girls in the mid-1950s, with Miss Marjorie Talbot (front, centre), the headmistress.

Staff of Nuneaton's Maypole dairy shop in Nuneaton in the 1950s, when rationing was still in force.

Employees of Courtaulds Ltd, Marlborough Road, Nuneaton, who received long-service awards in June 1952.

Long-service award recipients at Sterling Metals, Nuneaton, pictured in April 1970.

Staff at Nuneaton Co-operative Society's shop in Whittleford Road, Stockingford, in June 1952.

Staff at the Department of Inland Revenue, in Wheat Street, Nuneaton, in June 1953.

Geoffrey Johnson Smith interviews Councillor Bob Chamberlain outside Nuneaton Council House on October 14, 1957 for BBC Television. It followed BBC's *Tonight* programme which carried a controversial feature on Nuneaton, filmed by Slim Hewitt, in which he severely criticised Nuneaton.

Nuneaton Sea Cadets in the 1960s who "abandoned ship" in 1970 when the unit was disbanded. It was reformed in 1993...

...the Sea Cadets' headquarters, Training Ship Vanquisher, off Coventry Road, which was "sunk" to make way for a housing development.

On parade: Boys of the 121 (Nuneaton) Air Training Corps Squadron during an inspection in November 1967.

Nuneaton Army Cadets leave for a special parade in Ypres, Belgium, where their band headed a World War One memorial parade in May 1980.

Nuneaton Guides at a presentation ceremony in 1986.

Crowning of the May Queen in 1962. It is a ceremony that has been held at the Abbey Church, Nuneaton, for many years. On the left is the Vicar, the late Canon J.B.Sinker.

North-east Warwickshire Water Board at its inaugural meeting on March 16, 1960.
Back row (left to right): H.Greensmith, S.T.S.Walters, G.W.Pluck, F.L.Perkins, W.Bailey. Middle row: R.W.Stain, C.W.Campling, R.Hadden, D.Underhill, R.L.Warren, J.I.Evans, J.W.Fletcher, J.Sanders, L.Ford. Seated: M.R.Moreton, H.Kelsey, J.Allen, E.Bond, H.A.Corbett, G.Ashton (engineer and manager), A.A.Crabtree (clerk), E.J.Lewis (treasurer) and L.N.Anderton.

Mayor Jack Warren presides over the final meeting of the old Nuneaton Borough Council before its merger with Bedworth Urban District Council in 1974. Leslie Huckfield MP (front, centre) is sitting behind Bill Olner, who was to become MP 18 years later.

Nuneaton and Bedworth's champion Town Crier, Paul Gough.

One of Nuneaton's best-known characters Daisy McBean (later Haynes), who died in 1995, was the town's charity champion. The Jamaican-born former nurse lived in the town for 37 years and was a familiar sight in pubs, clubs and shops as well as at the annual carnival rattling a tin for charity. She received the MBE from the Queen for her charity work in 1993.

Ken Loach, Nuneaton's film-making pioneer. The Nuneaton Old Edwardian rose to fame when he directed *Kes* in 1969 and he has since made a number of other films, each with thought-provoking messages.

Nurses, who took part in a sponsored trolley-push around Nuneaton in 1980, hand over £150 to Anker Radio chairman Terry Hancock. The hospital broadcasting service for many years operated from a portable building in a car park, but in 1995 moved into new studios at the maternity hospital block.

Eyes left: Nuneaton Old Edwardians at a reunion smile at two girl students. King Edward VI Grammar (founded 1552) was an all-boys school until the education re-organisation programme in the 1970s.

Caring Nuneaton... health chairman Geoffrey Jackson receives the keys to a mini bus for Bramcote Hospital, presented by the town's most successful fund-raising charity, the League of Friends. The League has raised thousands of pounds over the years to buy hospital equipment and comforts for patients. Its most successful project was launched in 1993 with the Scanner Appeal for the George Eliot Hospital. Within 14 months more than £365,000 was raised, most of it coming from the people of Nuneaton, Bedworth, Atherstone and Hinckley.

Consultants Michael Cox (centre) and Vic Kenyon (right) with crane operator Roy Williams are given a bird's eye view of the multi-million pound development at George Eliot Hospital in 1991. The new-look hospital was officially opened by the Queen in December 1994.

The Coat of Arms 'United to Achieve' – which became the borough's symbol after the amalgamation of Nuneaton and Bedworth in 1974.